IN THE COUNTRY

IN THE

Inge Morath

A Studio Book

COUNTRY

Arthur Miller

The Viking Press · New York

First published in 1977 by The Viking Press
625 Madison Avenue, New York, N.Y. 10022

Published simultaneously in Canada by
The Macmillan Company of Canada Limited

Text and black-and-white photographs printed in
the United States of America

Color photographs printed in Japan

Library of Congress Cataloging in Publication Data

Morath, Inge.
In the country.

(A Studio book)
1. Connecticut—Description and travel—1951-
Views. 2. Country life—Connecticut—Pictorial works.
I. Miller, Arthur, 1915-   II. Title.
F95.M64   974.6'04   76-53842
ISBN 0-670-39678-8

To Rebecca

1

Born and raised in city apartments, it was always a marvel to me that people lived in separate houses they could walk around, where they could lean out of a window and touch a tree branch, decide to take out a wall and extend a room, enter and leave without taking an elevator, be free to pound around on the floor without the tenants below banging on their ceiling with a broomstick. Later, the concept of eating what one had planted, of causing a landscape to change—the idea of the countryside itself— was oddly like that of the theater, an arena one's presence could change and shape, while the city was concrete and repelled the touch of the hand with its indifference. Others had made the city; a place of one's own waited on its creator.

One winter day in the late 1940s I drove northward in the borrowed truck of a friend who ran an apple orchard to look over a house put up for sale by a business- man, the boss of another friend. A phenomenal snowfall a few days earlier had left the back country roads lined with walls of snow piled higher than a car, blanking out all but an occasional glimpse of the rolling hills. Without a road map and thoroughly lost, I came over the top of a ridge and was descending when I saw a car parked at the bottom of the dip, its door opening, and a gray-haired man emerging carrying two large grocery bags. My wheels locked and I slid down and banged into the car, sending the man sprawling and his groceries skidding in all directions. I got out, apologized, and, while helping him to retrieve his canned goods and in an attempt to take his mind off the accident, asked him for directions to Mr. ——'s house. Inevitably, he was the

7

owner I was looking for. He had had trouble with a slipped disc for years, and his fall required him to do some calisthenics, which added to my burden of guilt as we discussed the plumbing, the heating, and the boundaries of his forty-four acres. The snow outside was nearly waist high and the path he had cut to the front door merely led out to the road, so it was impossible to see the house in its setting. Worse, the roof was loaded with so much snow that even its true outlines were beyond imagining. All I knew was that it looked beautiful, isolated, and in very good shape, and that he was asking only twenty-one thousand dollars, including the clay tennis court whose tall fence I could actually see through the back-porch door. With the hope of a bank loan and the prospect of alleviating his intensifying pain, I shook hands on the deal, with which he arose from the floor. Back in the city, I waited for a sign of the sun coming out and the melting which would let me have a look at what I had bought.

On the first warming day I hurried back and there it was, a small farmhouse much too close to a four-cornered road intersection but otherwise perfect. I lived there for ten summers, and the only traffic was a neighboring farmer's truck occasionally going by and the mailman's car.

Early that spring my first confrontation with nature began. The trees were still lifeless and bare, but one giant had a hairy vine winding up and around its trunk. One does not truly own a thing until one has changed it, and so I proceeded to own the tree by tearing the vine off with my bare hands. Later that afternoon, eating a sandwich in the sun, the first itching began on my belly. By evening it was under my arms and at around four o'clock in the morning I was tearing at my flesh. The only relief was to stand under a scalding hot shower, a liquid equivalent of scratching. I have never walked in the country since without an eye automatically scanning the ground for poison ivy. It can be dangerous to approach nature sentimentally, and to do so in ignorance besides is distastrous. It may be taken as a rule that sentimentality toward nature increases with one's distance from contact with her. She simply bit back.

The township, a vast territory, had fewer than seven hundred and fifty voters in those days and I knew not one of them. And if over the past twenty-five years, fifteen of which I have spent in the country year-round, I have come to know a few, I have no illusion that we share the same culture. At the same time, the differences between city and country man have, I realize now, been swiftly vanishing in precisely this period.

Three hours from New York City in those days, and with super-highways an hour closer now, the area in the late forties still had farmers who recalled shoveling a path through snow for miles cross-country, followed by the team and wagon filled with

8

milk cans. In a district settled since the 1700s they lived in houses like the one I live in, without a closet, and in a lifetime had never traveled farther than forty miles from home. I still have the arched-lidded trunks in which generations kept their few good clothes and the linens. One of these people, a fellow named Bob Tracy, was born in that first house I bought, but it was something he never mentioned until we had known each other for two or three years.

In fact, it had as little significance for him as the fact that his family name showed up on deeds of thousands of acres of land, while he lived now on an acre down in a gully where the postmaster, a part-time mason with an enormous wen on the left hinge of his jaw, had built him a cinder-block cabin. "Well," he explained one time, "I had six sisters, don't y'know, and whenever one of 'em wanted a new hat they'd sell twenty acres." Now he did odd jobs for farmers, spelling them with the chores when they were sick or lazy or had to go off to a wedding or funeral, and mowed lawns for the few professional people around the township.

The interior of his cabin smelled, as the saying goes, like a bachelor on Friday, the atmosphere a mixture of kerosene, body sweat, and dog. More than once I had come on him asleep in his cot beside his dozing coonhound, Ella, the last remaining of three that he believed hunters from Waterbury had stolen. Awakened, he would clump out of bed pulling up his suspenders and, pretending the decency of surprise, would yell at the bitch to get out of the bed. She would open one eye and move a leg and go back to sleep and he would shake his head and say for the hundredth time, "Well they stole my *good* dogs, don't y'know," and glare back at Ella as though it were her fault.

He must have been in his late fifties then, a thin but hard-bodied man with crinkly eyes and a mum mouth that he could press shut when listening with skeptical amusement. He first stopped by on hearing a city man had bought a house, to ask if I had any junk I wanted to discard. Quickly catching on to my penchant for never throwing anything away if I can help it, he conceded, "Well, waste not, want not," and from then on we got along fine, for the profligate habits of the few city people he knew left him confused about their characters, and character for Bob and his kind was something like what television was later to become for millions of people—the most delicious amusement, a source of infinite interest, the chief escape from humdrum existence. Thinking of him now, and of the others of his generation, it seems to me that this sets them apart from those who followed them into a quite altered time. When you came by for a visit they sat back, and with a certain appetite, an eagerness born of much silence and few interruptions, seemed to wait like an audience for the curtain to rise and reveal something wonderful. With none of them did I ever sense that they

9

feared. It had nothing to do with bravery or nobility, but was simply a confidence that the man before them had an existence worth looking into.

Every item in Bob's cabin had either been given to him as junk or rescued from the town dump. Except, of course, for his rifle and three shotguns standing on their butts against a wall, shining and clean. On an up-ended crate stood a two-burner kerosene stove and an iron frying pan with a deep layer of yellow grease that had probably not been disturbed since the first Roosevelt administration. The longer I knew him, the more likely it seemed that if he were to wake one morning and find himself living at the turn of the eighteenth century, he would have needed less than ten minutes to feel at home, and much more so than he did now, as the 1950s were beginning. For one thing, he could never understand why people discarded cars, refrigerators, furniture, pots and pans that were still perfectly usable, reminder of an age when people spent a large amount of time repairing things. Once, inspecting a new car I had just bought, he turned to me and asked, "How long you going to keep it?" The question was pure, without irony; he was trying to understand what objects meant to people like me, for in his mind we sort of rented what we possessed.

Useless as a carpenter, he would nervously consent to steady one end of a board while I nailed the other. Once when I stood back to admire my work, and asked for his opinion, which I hoped would be positive, he asked, "How long you going to keep this place?" It bewildered him that people bought places, rushed about for two or three years redoing them, planting new trees and shrubs, and suddenly one morning were loading everything into a moving van—divorced, or changing states on orders from their companies. Finally he thought he understood the rationale: "It improves the countryside anyway."

One day early in our acquaintance when he was helping me to set posts for a fence around the new vegetable garden, he said, "I hear you write movies."

"Not movies, plays. For the stage."

"Oh!—those old-fashioned shows. Where they put them on?"

"New York."

"Well now—I didn't know they still had them."

At the approach of any female he removed his hat and pressed it against his chest, and his face turned pink. He would wash the outsides of windows but not the insides and the cellar stairs only to the top step, past which point he might find himself trapped inside a house with a woman. Anyway, inside a house was "woman's work," which he did not so much disdain as fear he would be criticized for doing badly, and to face a woman criticizing him was as close to dying as a man could come this side of the grave itself.

12

Through his eyes I saw the countryside emerging from its anonymity. Not far from his cabin, the one-room schoolhouse still stands, surrounded with old lilac bushes, a space twenty by thirty feet where he had gone to school as a boy along with the children of nearly every family for miles around. So they came to know each other's kinks and habits from the beginning and what to expect from them as adults.

"This Donald Price. When he grew up he come to run the general store. Old Donald was always on the lookout for a trick to play on y'. Well, there was this Mrs. Croker used to have him deliver everything, never would carry a bag out of the store herself. This one time he delivered the groceries and she says to him, 'I forgot a spool of white thread, Donald, would you bring it by if you don't mind.' Well, Donald thought about that and says to her, 'You want one spool of white thread delivered?' And she says that is what she wanted.

"So he goes back to his store, and they had this great big wagon for delivering lumber and a team pullin' it. So he hitches up the team, and sets this spool right on the bed and drives over to Mrs. Croker's and knocks on the door and she opens up and he says, 'I have your thread, where do you want it?' And he goes back to the wagon and pulls out these two heavy planks they used to roll down barrels on, and sets them on the tail of the wagon, and doesn't he roll that spool down the planks and picks it up on his shoulder like it weighed two hundred pounds and staggers up to her porch and sets it carefully right next to her feet. And that was that."

The World War II years were the best in his life. If he had a profession, it was hunting red fox, worth a dollar a pelt, if it had not yet been destroyed by rabies. Walking a dirt road he would point to the crotch of a tree where twenty-five years earlier he had rested his gun and gotten three big ones. His mind was filled with pictures of encounters on the roads.

"About midnight once, I's coming down this road looking for fox, and off ahead I hear this sound, *zoo, zoo, zoo,* like somebody sawing. No wind at all, and a full moon you could read your paper by. Well, I stood still listening, and sure enough it sound just like somebody sawing up ahead in the middle of night. So I come around the turn and there's this Pollack—they used to live in your house—and he's sawing this horse's head off right there in the middle of the road. It'd dropped dead there that afternoon and he was taking him apart to feed the pigs. They'd cut a hole in the kitchen floor and'd drop food down to the pigs in the cellar when it was winter. They certainly were peculiar people."

He parted the brush beside a road one day to show the remains of a stone foundation where he claimed an inn once stood, and beside it a blacksmith shop. "All the kids'd come and sit right here and watch the people getting out of the stage from

The organic gardener.

The knife-sharpening man.

Overleaf: *By courtesy of the druggist.*

Litchfield. This was the busiest spot around.'' I doubted a stage was still running in what must have been the nineties, but he insisted. ''One time two robbers held them up and ran off with a bag of gold from the bank. They caught them, but they never found the money. It's buried up back on your land if you ever want to go look for it.'' I said I'd go half with him if he looked for it, and he burst out laughing, but it was still hard to tell how much of a spoof it was. Keeping a straight face was one of life's pleasures, and like his friends he cultivated a talent for Yankee one-liners.

Albert, the local state trooper, had been repeatedly warning Bob that it was illegal for him to be selling junk without a license. The weeds around his cabin were studded with burned-out vacuum cleaners, rusted gears, refrigerators, lawn mowers, and the first thing he did each morning when he came out the door on his way to the brook where he took his bath was to run his eye over his treasures to see if anything had been stolen during the night. Paying the license fee, about ten dollars, was bad, but his real reluctance was to have his name written down on any government register. This was why he refused a job as a grounds keeper at a nearby private school. ''They make you put in for that social security, you know, and you got to sign for that. Next thing they'll be after me for the income tax.'' So he took care to cover whatever he was taking to the junkyard with burlap bags until someone gave him a derelict truck. Piece by piece he transported the vehicle to the junkyard, but at last he was down to the long rear axle housing, which there was no way to conceal—the end of it stuck out several feet from under his trunk lid.

He decided to take the chance, however, and set out with it for Waterbury. On his way he stopped off for bread, and coming out of the store he saw Albert standing behind his car staring down at the protruding axle. Selling auto parts without a license is especially frowned on, ''So I knew I was in for it now. Well, I couldn't do much about it and I walk over to him and he looks at me and says, 'Hi, Bob.' And I says, 'Hi, Albert.' And he says, 'Nice day.' And I says, 'It was.' ''

His class consciousness was stubborn, a reminder of a long-gone populism very much at odds with the new wisdom of the fifties, when the intellectual centers were busy announcing the end of ideology and the imminent disappearance of the American poor. The system's only remaining problem, they said, was to save itself and the world from Communism, while internally we need only rely on the automatic spreading of infinite riches to everybody. Bob read the only available local newspaper with its prideful Republican slant, never missing the local newscasts on his radio, a thirties model shaped like a cathedral. He ended up supporting Henry Wallace for President, a candidate favored by the Left who piled up a full one million votes against Truman.

20 ''He's the only one I can understand,'' he would say, but the real reason was that

most people hated and feared Wallace as a menace. In his mind these were the same kinds of people who kept pushing for stricter zoning regulations requiring three-acre lots around any new house. "They just don't want the working man living around here," was his interpretation. From where he sat, the prospect was weird; "You be turning it all into a park." The land, he meant, which had always been a place of work and working men.

Through his vision of the land, the picturesque tended to disintegrate into long-forgotten purposes that had once created its aesthetic. The New England landscape is partitioned by patterns of stone walls, lichen-painted and enduring. Originally, they were convenient dumps for the rocks cleared from the fields they enclose that otherwise could not be planted. I was dismantling a section of wall one day when he came by in his bouncing Olds that stalled a few yards away. Its gasoline pump had died a year or so earlier and above the engine he had hung a Mazola can with a rubber tube from an enema bag leading to the carburetor. We got to talking about walls.

"My grandfather built your wall. A man and a team of oxen could do a rod of fence a day. That's the fence that nearly got him in the Civil War."

"How come?"

"Well, he was a real small man, and he's out here building this wall, and this squad of cavalry come riding down the road here conscripting men for the army, and they catch sight of him working here. But my grandmother was out behind the house, and she heard the horses and come running. She was a tremendous woman, and don't she pick up my grandfather and set him on her hip and says, 'You can't take my boy!' That saved him cause they wouldn't take boys helping their mothers."

Talking of war, he was reminded of Ben Fitzer. Fitzer was in his nineties during World War I, a farmer in this secluded valley who rarely even came into town. "But this one time, he come in for some reason, and this fellow come over to him and says, 'Isn't it awful all those men killing each other by the millions?' It was the first beautiful day of spring and old Fitzer says, 'What men you mean killing each other?' And the fellow says, 'Over in Europe, Ben. There's a terrible big war going on over there.' 'Well,' says Fitzer, 'they got a nice day for it.'"

Speaking of isolated people reminded him of the two unmarried brothers who had once lived in my house. "They were real churchgoers, don't y'know, went down there every Sunday. And around about January or so they didn't show up. Then next Sunday come and they're not there either. Finally, after they hadn't been for three Sundays, a committee was appointed to go up and see if there's anything wrong. Well, they come up the house and knock, and the door opens, and there's one of them, and they goes inside and asks why they hadn't been to church all month. And he says his brother'd died and he didn' feel he ought to leave him. 'Ought to leave him! Why? Where is he?' 'In the front room,' he says. And sure enough, they go over to the parlor, and there he's got him laid out on two sawhorses and a board. 'I'm waitin' for the thaw,' he says. That'll give you an idea how cold these houses were.''

He would go through seizures of business acumen, especially on hearing how somebody had gotten thousands of dollars for a few acres. In the late forties when I arrived, land was sold with a wave of the arm indicating the bounds, and it was so cheap, around forty dollars an acre, worth three or four thousand fifteen years later, that the "more or less" on the contract could often leave the purchaser with fifteen acres when he had paid for ten. By the sixties, when the farms were being transformed into residences, ledgy back pastures that had hardly had a money value were discovered to have a view, and surveyors were popping up in the brushy woods with their transits and stakes, marking off lines as though an inch either way mattered greatly. Bob would suddenly show up in my yard trying to incarnate himself into a canny businessman. "Sell y' my whole place including the house for six thousand dollars,'' he said one day.

"What the hell would I do with it?''

"Sell it. Make yourself a profit. My cabin's *quiet,* it's *secluded*''—he had picked up the real-estate jargon by now but spoke it uncertainly, as if it were some foreign language—"nice running brook, too.''

"In August?''

"Well hell, *nothin'* runs in August.'' I expected the usual mock-innocent spoofing look, but his humor was no longer in his eyes. Instead, he actually seemed to be waiting for me to begin dealing about his miserable house and his damp and weedy gully, and his face showed an avidity I had never seen in him before. It was as though suddenly we were adversaries—he wanted what I had, and I was refusing what he had to offer. Our bantering connection was over with; he was trying to clamber aboard the great American Train and resenting me as though I were stamping on his fingers.

We would meet on the road after that but he hardly paused. He sold his place and moved in with a retired bachelor, Dr. Steele, whose estate he tended, a miserly watcher of oil stocks, and they argued a lot, I heard. Years passed. I had forgotten about him entirely, when from my car window I spotted him mowing a lawn in front of the home of Mrs. Tyler, a divorced nurse. He had occasionally worked for her years before when we were still friends, and one time she had left a note for him on her door listing his chores, all of them to be accomplished in the two hours she paid him. "Dear Bob,'' 23 it read, "please mow the lawn, put up the storm windows, clean out the flower beds, sweep out the garage, and take the garbage to the dump." Bob studied the list, then took out the stub of a pencil from his shirt pocket and carefully inscribed below, "Dear Mrs. Tyler, my ears are not that long, yrs, Bob," and never went back.

I stopped my car and called to him. It was good to see the grin that broke out on his face when he looked up. He stopped the mower, came over, and stood beside the car. It was hot, and his shirt was off, and it was a shock to see hanging flesh on his once tight-skinned body. His Irish blue eyes seemed to be shrouded by an unhealthy gray wetness. The old shyness seemed like shame now. Our paths had been crossing for nearly twenty-five years, and this was the first time in his presence that the thought of failure struck my mind. He was grinning, but his impishness had gone to bitterness in the curl of his mouth. As he came close, I could smell beer. He had never drunk enough to smell in daytime. His swollen-knuckled hands, the fingers arthritically curved, the faint wheezing of breath in his chest all sent me back to the day long ago when, teaching me to scythe, he had grasped the snath, and, trading his weight from leg to leg, his eyes fixed in a pleasurable glaze, he had circled half an acre, leaving behind a swath of smooth lawn, and returned to me hardly winded.

"You working for her again?"

"Well, she's not too bad."

"How's it going with Dr. Steele?"

"Oh, he's dead."

"I hadn't heard. When'd he die?"

"Oh, it's over a year now," he said, and then he glanced carefully up and down the empty road and leaned down to me, and lowering his voice, he confided, "Won't be missed."

The mum, mock-proper mouth and the wicked eye were suddenly there again, and we laughed, and for an instant we were back the way it had been before he had learned caution, before all the land had become real estate and when his own kind were still on the farms around him and he was at home and free to savor whatever flew from his mouth.

He died a few months later, alone in a room he had taken over a tavern in town facing the railroad tracks. It was surprising to learn he had reached eighty. Then it was possible that he had sat by the inn as a boy to watch the passengers dismounting from the stage.

24

Mutual aid.

Farmer, former merchant seaman, with half a mind to pack his duffel bag again, what with the astronomical prices of fertilizer and equipment and the roller-coaster changes in milk price. "Half the world's starving and they tell us we're making too much milk. The trouble with farmers is they love to farm. If they loved it less maybe it would force the politicians to start making sense of this idiotic business."

The late Percy Beardsley with photos of his prize-winning oxen. In World War I he was the famed Sergeant York's corporal. Asked if it was really true that York had single-handedly outfought and captured a whole German company, he answered, "Well y'know, they'd started fighting way back in nineteen-fourteen, and we only came over in seventeen, so by that time they were pretty tired." In his coal cellar were barrels of apple cider and brandy decades old, powerful stuff. An elbow-length mummified white kid glove covered with gray dust lay on one barrel, its fingers drooping toward the bung. This was the "Norma Shearer barrel," she having left the glove there in the twenties when they shot scenes for a movie on his place. It was forbidden to disturb the glove. He only married in his sixties, the shivaree lasting through a weekend. A wavering guest having upset a bottle of bourbon, Percy turned to him in his grave, deliberate way, saying, "I'd rather see a church burn than waste good whisky."

He had a world reputation as a trainer of oxen, with the calligraphic touch of a switch made them move as delicately as dancers. The government had him training teams for India. In the old days with his father, he drove his teams down the roads by night, twenty-five miles to Danbury to compete in the Fair. His father, in his eighties, had few teeth and munched on raw clams from his jacket pocket. They had an immense collection of hats—derbies, western stetsons, straws, caps, twenty or thirty which hung on meathooks from the living-room beams. Asked why, he said, "I like them." His land is unused now, the broad, sloping pastures going for building lots.

*There has been but one name on the deed to the place since the first
Hurlbutt came over the ridge in the sixteen hundreds to clear space for
a house. Inside is a tall tripod carrying rifles borne by Hurlbutts back
to King Philip's War and down through every war Americans have
fought. An amazing range of crops here—sweet corn, potatoes, many
varieties of apple, pear, cherry, peach; chickens and eggs, duck, capon,
geese, pigs, and sheep, one of them being shorn right now. He recently
discovered a minister, car parked right out on the road not far from
the house, stealing apples off one of his trees. He laughs, telling about*

it, offered the man all he could carry. An educated family that has always been involved in town affairs. But the farm will most certainly vanish with him—it makes little sense to work this hard. In a society without an idea of a consummation, he has only his affection: for family, the land, the town; and it is often not enough. When everybody is too busy to tend the roadside stand, he leaves a jar on the counter full of change; the customer helps himself and drops what is owed into the jar. The unguarded money dumbfounds foreigners and most city people, yet it is rarely stolen, although produce occasionally disappears.

Baptism of father's amazing new hay bale-throwing machine which, it turns out, works.

Professor and granddaughter.

The war on the woodchucks.

Overleaf: *Democrats' picnic.*

2

Facing the state highway, the house looks rather elegant nowadays, a large colonial with a sloping lawn on three sides and a new white fence and a Mercedes in the driveway. In the other time it was Gussie's, and the clapboards were curling, the roof had lost some of its wood shingles, and there was always a high pile of firewood beside the kitchen door. Even in her great age, she'd be out there in the winter splitting logs with an ax, a stringy woman with a tangle of long white hair and a piercing scream in her voice. But all this was only the joke of age; underneath was a life-abounding woman who had a way of confronting a man, sizing him up for what he might be good for.

Way back before the roads were paved and a house like this commonly had a single cold-water faucet and a six-foot-long claw-footed bathtub, Gussie had been a young farmer's wife and they had a hired man. After a while she had gotten to like the hired man, and one evening around the porcelain-topped kitchen table the three of them agreed that her husband ought to leave, and he and Gussie got a divorce and she married the hired man. Six or seven years later, the husband returned to visit and spent the night. They were glad to see him again and talk over old times, and the next day they hardly had time for the chores, there was so much to say. They really were glad to be together again. After a few weeks Gussie realized that she had made a mistake, so she broached the subject around the kitchen table, and they all agreed that the hired man–husband would be better off leaving. She got a divorce from him and was back with her first husband again.

A number of years passed, she found it hard to remember exactly how many, and the hired man, who had been working in Boston, stopped by one Sunday to visit. Gussie and her husband were glad to see him, and he stayed the night and all next day told about what he had been doing in the years they had been apart, and Gussie got to like him again. By this time, however, they were all in their late fifties, so it seemed foolish to bother with a divorce and the three of them settled in together. Gussie cooked and the men farmed, and she would be faithful to one for many months at a time, and to the other for months too. In his middle sixties her husband died—that is, her first husband—and she was left with the hired man.

One night—they were in their seventies about this time—the house of a neighboring artist caught fire. He was one of Gussie's particular favorites because he often stopped on his way to town to ask if she needed anything, and was always glad to talk. She and the hired man were getting ready for bed when the artist phoned and asked if she could put up a guest of his for the night, the fire having ruined her room, and

Gussie was delighted with her unaccustomed role as hostess. The guest, a lady turning seventy, was bedded down on clean sheets in one of Gussie's many bedrooms, and just as she was about to reach over to turn out the light, her door opened softly and Gussie came in and went over to her on the bed and held out a table fork.

"Put this under your pillow," Gussie said, handing the fork to her guest.

"Why?" the amazed woman asked.

Gussie leaned down deep until the two old faces were inches apart. "You never can tell with these men," she whispered, snapped out the light, and left.

Overleaf: *Farm wedding: the end of the wayward sixties.*

Masonic Temple.

3

Until the mid-fifties, there was so little trading in land that the town clerk kept the deeds to every piece of property in a loose pile on top of his ancient desk by the window in his living room. He also ran a farm that bore no other name on its deed but his family's since it was first registered in the 1600s. In a corner of the living room stood a tall tripod with eight or ten rifles, from the World War II–Korea M1 Garand, at the bottom, to a five-foot-long muzzle-loader used in King Philip's War. Under each rifle was a brass plate with the name of the Hurlbutt who had borne it. He was about six feet six, a rather stately man who took his responsibilities very seriously. When I asked for my deed—a neighbor had been pleading for a couple of acres to move our boundary away from his kitchen door—Hurlbutt turned to the pile of deeds, and gently drew out mine. I wanted to be sure of my boundary line from which two acres could be calculated, and told this to him. Without glancing at the deed he described the landmarks, mainly a stone fence ending at the town road. "But your line slants east in his favor about twenty feet before it comes to the road so don't go by the fence all the way." He apparently had the bounds of every piece of land in the township in his head. Twenty years later, in his nineties, he spent all his days walking, mile on mile up and down the hills in the months before he died.

This territorial stability may have been peculiar to the area, more European, perhaps, than universally American. In Arkansas, once, on back roads around Fayetteville, almost every farm had a "For Sale" sign sticking out of the ground by the roadside. The signs looked weathered, their tilting posts half-rotted, and a friend who was taking me around explained that they were never removed. "They're always ready to sell. A lot of times they trade houses and just move a couple of thousand yards up the road while the neighbor is moving down to their house. There's the feeling it's always better somewhere else." It may be that the New Englanders who were more restless were the ones who went West, leaving behind the less adventurous, or perhaps those with no illusions that moving could save you.

Donated it to the
Historical Society,
decided to walk
it there.

Hunter.

Nanny: "When I'm engaged they've met their Waterloo."

Country welcome.

A midsummer night's dream.

Scholars waiting.

This dog, Hugo, saved lives by napping, in good weather, on the white line of the road outside his house. Expecting to find him there, people slowed down coming around the curve. He died, remarkably, of old age. A well-known traveler, he showed up on people's porches eight and ten miles away, would climb into the open door of any car, often discovered in the back seat only after hours of driving, but always showed pleasure on being returned. Suffered from reversal of instincts—would watch a rabbit go by, then rush in opposite direction looking for its hole, would spend half a day outside and come indoors to relieve himself, barked at strangers only when they were leaving, and mated only with poodles. Gentle with small children, from whom he stole food, ice cream, and dolls; terrified of the moon and falling rags. Faithless, morose, and unteachable, lived three years past normal maximum for his breed. Profound bell-toned voice. Only known use as companion to aged people at whose feet he could sit sharing the view entire afternoons.

Hugo.

Scholars working.

*Scholars
relieved.*

Scholars dating.

4

The dominant style of the buildings in this countryside is still that of the eighteenth century and its variants in the nineteenth, and this inherited imagery is the ground upon which a kind of unpremeditated discontinuity—even a surrealistic quality—emerges. The visible image is of a hard-headed, realistic people suspicious of fantasy, confined within utilitarian routines and a no-nonsense religion bare of ritual and vain show. But in fact, the people here are as often play-actors and far more fantastic than efficient; despite the legend, they live in an old country, and under the oldest continuous government on earth, with a past as mistily evocative as that of a European culture and countryside.

Nostalgia—that longing for a past shorn of its conflicts—is supported here by the physical reality, the remains and reconstructions of another time against which the people often seem like found objects, displaced persons, however prosperous some of them are. The woods, the house, barn, church, and streets evoke a pastoral simplicity, even as the farmers seen here, for example, plow and milk in the shadows of nuclear plants whose safety they have come to question; knowing too that the family farm itself is on its way to oblivion, and that they are survivors with a probably short future. As always, the camera sees the past—all it can see—and here it speaks of a symmetry of action and thought and a revolution based on empirical common sense, when in truth these people watch the television news for the event on Wall Street, in Washington or Korea that will affect the price of fertilizer and crops, regardless of their thoughts or planning. The surreal emerges from the fragility of what camera and mind can grasp as real.

So the pull of nostalgia is strong here, just as the face of the past is everywhere so evident. If some have fled cities, not to create the more human community but to deny a painfully intolerable present, others are renewed by a more ample space, cleaner air, the real contact with revolving seasons. Some don costumes of the past as though to mime a lost gentility, but others would simply rather drive to a factory job on a country road than buck traffic, and these can't help looking ahead for hope and not to a bygone time. In any case, they have created a style of life beyond the cities, and its vitality is in its contradictions as much as its consistencies.

"The face of the past is everywhere. . . ."

Fairs and debris.

Overleaf: *Church auction.*

Open-house day.

"Some of the great merchant houses, subsidized like great symphony orchestras, transform the American Revolution, like all others, into art."

Mark Twain's house.

Overleaf: *Riding instructress's couch.*

Nostalgia.

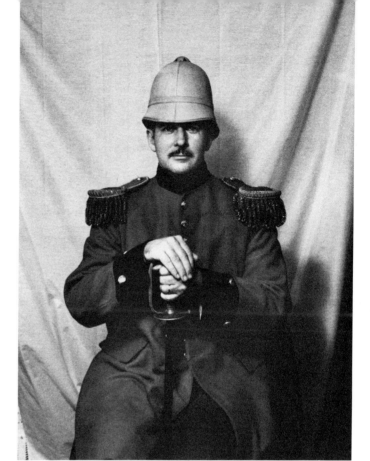

Horsing around with the nineties.

"Some don costumes of the past as though to mime a lost gentility."

5

It is a small garage and gas station, and like his predecessor, he refuses to expand it, despite the increase in business and population. "If I put in another lift, I have to have another man or two, and by the time I've paid them, I'm back where I am now." He used to be more cheerful before there were this many strangers. There is still not much traffic on the highway out front, and the small-town atmosphere remains, but there have been changes that he still finds hard to live with. "There were always people who couldn't pay on time. That's understandable, but it never was what you'd call a problem. At least it never bothered me, because there wasn't any question about their being straight with me. I mean, you can't be too hard on somebody just for being short.

"But it's nerve-racking now. They'll come in here, big station wagon, wife, kids, dog, the whole bit; educated people in executive positions; order four new tires and a complete tune-up, points, spark plugs, timing, the works. They drive off, and next thing I know, they've moved to Ohio or California. The thing is, some of them are real friendly, and they know in advance when they come in here that they're going to stiff me. I don't know what's got into people. It's got to where I have to try and size somebody up while I'm talking to him and decide if I trust him."

Some days he seems to find it hard to smile, and plods around chewing on a black Connecticut-made cigar, a man nearing fifty, living where he was born, but not at home any more.

The Steamboat Gothic commercial buildings seem designed to glamorize even if the plans come out of a carpenter's manual. A hundred years later, ironically, all its useless detail is comforting—as though somebody cared. Now the stamped-out storefronts so minimalize contact with the eye that it is hard to know which town's shopping street you're on, or which coat is yours.

Births, deaths, ripe scandals, secret ailments, imminent separations, reconciliations, bankruptcies, candidates for office, building plans, engagements, new and sundered friendships, bee stings, news of deer influxes, successful and failed operations, petitions to sign, election predictions, juvenile kleptomania, dawn thefts of newspapers by adults, waxing and waning of grudges, falling of wombs, stomachs, and arches, winning of scholarships, dyings at sea and at war, rescues from abandoned mineshafts, evidence of Mafia infiltrating, much irony, common sense and astonishment—in short, the drugstore.

*Hardware
theater.*

Carpenter-craftsman, figure skater, father of five, descendant of a revolutionary war general. "I must be stupid, but by God I still love to get up in the morning. I've only seen Germany and France, but I betcha this countryside'll match any spot in the world for beauty. I just wish I knew if we're ever going to get ourselves straightened out, though. I know I'm pretty ignorant, but I don't see how you can have a country if everybody is taught to honor the man who makes it with his mouth and look down his nose at the rest of us. I mean, how's it going to work if nobody knows how to do anything? There's only two men left I'd ever work with again; they know the trade and have good work habits. The rest of them just hold me back and tire me out watching for their mistakes. Although I must say I've come across a few long-haired young ones who are turning out pretty good, so maybe we'll come back to our senses at that. I hate to charge what I do, but even so by the end of the year I've just squeaked through. What gets me, though, is these people yelling, 'Labor, labor, the cost of labor.' Well, if it's so great to be labor, how come nobody wants to be it? You ever see a man stick his thumbs in his vest and boasting, 'Oh, my son is a carpenter!' Hell, no. A carpenter's lower than a bedbug. All and all, I guess I'm lucky to be doing the work I like. Not that a whole lot of people know the difference between good work and bad, but I know and I guess that's the main thing. I read the other day about these Chinese making everybody put in time, out with the peasants. Not that I believe the government ought to tell people what to do, but there's something in that, you know? Maybe if some of these upper echelons had to mix with the common people, things'd start making some sense again. Although I guess something else'll foul it up. Well, it's one beautiful day today anyway, and I'm still breathing, so I guess I'm ahead."

Public notices.

6

When the hippie movement began in the sixties, and the floundering toward the commune life, it reminded me that this conservative town was established by a breakaway segment of a long-settled congregation on the other side of the ridge. They had a different idea of how to treat with God. The names given so many New England places enhance the impression of an age-old American quest for grace through a more perfect or more unified spiritual community: Bethel, Canaan, Goshen, Bethlehem are not saints but mythically hallowed communities. Of course, the mother colony at Plymouth, Massachusetts, was originally set up as a commune where for some years afterward the leadership appointed each person to certain chores and duties, where an individual was not allowed simply to venture out and begin cultivating land beyond the defensible bounds. A uniformity of modest dress, not much different from that currently found in China, a social discipline that forbade pursuits useless or hostile to the community, it was a vision of the sublime harmony of man's community and God. The triumph of the vision was the devoted sharer in the common enterprise rather than the individual free personality; the saint serves. With time and a surplus, this discipline justified by deprivation weakened and the commune was fractured into its family cells, each living for itself on separate land holdings. Beneath its sublimity, the whole concept could not have been improved on as an economic design in a hostile land.

The creation of latter-day communes by middle-class sons and daughters who can phone home for money has suffered the fictional unreality of privation self-willed rather than given. These young people have fled from surplus and privilege where their models sought escape from want and from senselessly denied opportunity. The quest for community shows no sign of dying, however, not permanently at any rate, on this landscape where it was nearly realized and wholly forgotten many times. The stark, simple wooden churches with their discreet ornamentation are like shards of a lost comity whose meaning is now read through the mists of nostalgia—a yearning for a vanished individualism—when they signify, in truth, the direct opposite. This pristine architecture celebrates not the loner freed of communal obligation, not man in a state of unacknowledged war with his fellows, but the ideal of mutuality and its suspicion of worldliness. The buildings are now seen most commonly with sentimentality, although they were designed like arrows pointed toward the rocky road littered with the baggage of the world and its illusions.

Death and transfiguration.

7

In the early fifties when Senator Joe McCarthy was at his most exuberant and whatever inanity he chose to utter was published as gospel by the press, my name would be mentioned from time to time as one of the suspicious radicals in the entertainment world, and I began to notice some intensely curious stares in the hardware store. The area had been conservative Republican since that party's beginnings, and a liberal was somebody who, perhaps, thought some of the rotted guardrail posts along the roads should be replaced before rather than after they leaned over by themselves and fell down. With nothing that could be called hard evidence, it was still easy to feel like a minority of one, and Tocqueville's observation more than a century earlier that the American wanted above all to move with the majority seemed as apt as ever.

When McCarthy could insinuate that a pillar of rectitude such as General of the Army George Catlett Marshall was part of the international Communist Apparatus without causing a storm of disgust, but merely several discreet and ineffectual demurrers, and when one witnessed otherwise sane and decent people seriously discussing the General's treason instead of the Senator's mental stability, it seemed time to write "Canceled" over the whole American democratic experiment.

Addressing the nation one night on television, the Senator, in a fit of well-earned confidence as to the result, challenged anyone to say that he had ever spoken a lie. As for myself, I had no doubt of the cowed silence which turned out to be the national response the next day. But by evening, the radio reporters were leading off their news summaries with an incredible item: a Mrs. Dooley of Roxbury, Connecticut, had fired off a telegram offering to demonstrate that the Senator had indeed told some lies. It was the sole response from the people of the United States.

I happened to be working outside my house next morning when I heard a tractor approaching around the curve in the road, and on it was a farmer, Joe Dooley, the lady's husband, drawing a manure spreader behind the machine. I waved him to a stop and asked if it had been his wife who had wired the Senator. I would hardly have expected the Dooleys, good Catholics and farmers, to throw down the gauntlet to the stereotyped thinking of the time. Joe laughed from his tractor seat, and over the pounding of the two-cylinder John Deere he shouted down at me, "Oh, it was her, all right. We thought he had gone too fur!" and letting in the clutch, he drove down the road.

With the influx of city people over the next years, the Democratic vote climbed, and Mrs. Dooley became head of the Democratic Town Committee and a town official. Her telegram, of course, was never answered. Again, the incident reminded me of how much harder it is to stand apart in the country than in the city, where you melt into the crowd. The country nonconformist can look to few allies and has no place to hide. He does have the land he stands on, however, and when female Irish combativeness and wit are thrown into the mixture, some wild surprises can explode.

Jackey Dooley with her first Selectman.

Some towns still have fairs. Once upon a time, when people were stuck to the farm most of the year, these must have been a big bang. Now, professionally entertained on television every night, the customers come to be amused by amateurism, creaky rides, undeodorized animal smells, competitions between breed fanciers, and other evidences of a life that was not yet packaged. A pleasing nostalgia, but the man currying the sheep might be a computer expert in real life.

The art is to maneuver the team, backing them together up to the sledge bearing thousands of pounds of concrete slabs, then quickly hooking them on and shouting them forward in unison. If one is a step behind the other at the breakaway, the combined force is split in half and the contest is lost along with the whole year's work of training.

The Near West.

Main Street.

The Fire Department.

Warriors.

*Strangers far
from home.*

8

As the farms vanished and the old houses were renovated by new owners, a class of contractors and artisans proliferated, made up of farmers' sons in good part. He was a good house painter, quick and hard-working, and especially trustworthy on ladders and painting church steeples, from which he hung on rope chairs. Tall and boyishly lanky, he found he could charm some customers, among them a few who were wealthy and successful and yet treated him, he felt, with the respect due an artist. Theirs were not just houses but homes, and he was trusted to move some extremely precious things. Now and then he would be invited in by the lady of the house for coffee or even a drink at quitting time. He took to reading best sellers and discussed them with these people, who were often surprised that a man in paint-flecked overalls knew something of culture. By the end of his twenties it had become difficult to abide the thought of another day with a paintbrush; having worked on some of the houses remodeled by artists from the city, he longed to live as they did, creating and being paid for it. This was freedom, and the only life he wanted any more.

To raise money for the Fire Department, they will dress up in old-time costumes and re-create old stores. Some of the faces look just right.

He tried writing some of the stories he had lived through in the Navy during the war, but he had trouble with grammar. Amazing adventures evaporated under his pencil. He bought a typewriter, but it did not seem to shorten his endless sentences. With no one around to advise him, he went to New York and enrolled in a writing school, paid several hundred dollars for the course, and received incomprehensible evaluations of his work. On one of his trips, he met a Cuban girl who was standing in the bus station and seemed lost. He had learned some Spanish in Cuba and decided to try to help her. He enjoyed helping people, and when he managed to do so, his face became boyish with pleasure. He bought the girl a hot dog and a Coke, and they walked around in the city. By the end of the afternoon, he found it hard to think of leaving her to the mercy of the city whose language she could not even speak. So he found her a room in a midtown hotel, but returned home worrying about her so much that he felt he loved her. Within a few weeks they were married, and he brought her back to his little town. She was a rather meek girl who believed in him completely, and his ambition as an artist became even more urgent.

He began to feel dizzy on high ladders, and the smell of paint made him nauseated. Once his throat closed up and he could hardly breathe, but the doctor could find nothing wrong. His contractor, finding him one day clinging to a gutter two stories up, had to go up and help him to the ground. A nervous trill had crept into his voice; a certain childishness seemed to be coming over him. Although his father had died or disappeared when he was an infant, he would refer to him now and then as though he were alive in the town. One day he started to lift a full can of paint and couldn't straighten up. The doctor advised a few days on his back, but even after two weeks he felt sharp pain. He applied for his compensation insurance and began receiving checks. Then there began an endless series of medical re-examinations by insurance company doctors who could neither locate the source of his pain nor order his payments ended. In his late forties or early fifties now, he lives on his insurance, the boyish look fixed on his face, and he turns his head as though his neck were in a cast. He is affable and pleasant, but when he meets one of the artists on the street or in the grocery, a look of open hunger floods his face, his eyes come alive with some distant whisper of guilt, his words come in a rush, and he talks about a story he has written, starting to tell the plot. They sigh, he notices it, and unable to bring himself to openly ask them to save him somehow, some way, he ends in a sweat of apology for detaining them and hurries back to his car. The best days of his year are the three during the Firemen's Fair when he can put on his blue fireman's cap and oversee the ring-tossing booth. Here he is his old self again, with a job to do that everyone respects and understands has to be done. Busy from early morning until past midnight, on these three days he doesn't have to write at all, and for the first two or three Fairs people begin to think he has come back to himself. Still, when the booths are taken down and the tents folded, something like guilt returns, and the hunger is there in his eyes.

Overleaf: *Calder changing the landscape.*

Garden party.

Previous Page: *Pilobolus dance group rehearsal. Straight-faced and insane,
they test the outer limits of gravity and the suggestibility of the onlooker's mind.*

Country Club:
Fourth of July.

The interpreters.

9

They had agreed upon an arrangement, not uncommon in these families, that whoever would agree to take care of mother could have the farm. One by one the two brothers and three sisters married and left the house, and Bert, the youngest son, remained there with Mrs. Tanner. He was forty then, and she in her early sixties.

He would have had reason to believe he had made a good deal. There were a hundred and fifty acres of open pasture around the house and farther back another eighty that were ledgy and rock-strewn but good enough for grazing. For a hundred and seventy-five years this house and land had kept the same family respectable. 137

But whether it was Bert's fixation on his mother or economics, he never married, and when she died in her nineties he found himself sole owner of a beautifully situated house, barns, and forty head of cows—in effect, a milk-producing apparatus that in its essentials was altered little from what it had been for nearly two centuries. Within a few months of his mother's death, he sold out and retired to Florida. In his sixties now, he saw no reason to continue getting up at four in the morning to milk cows when he could clear more cash by selling out than he would ever live to see as a farmer. And in the two days I spent with him tracing the bounds in the woods out back, looking under the brush for signs of rotted wooden criss-cross fences, he never showed a sign of sentimental regret. He was a short man and mild. He met my inquiries about the life in former times with a shy embarrassment, as though he wanted to escape identity with what was old-fashioned and foolish. Farming was for people who hadn't managed to escape it and nobody with any brains worked that hard. By selling the place and retiring he was joining the winners and leaving the losers behind. Each time we stopped to talk in the scraggly woods he took out a Lucky from the pack in his breast pocket. When he got back to the empty house he complained of pain in his back, which he thought he had twisted. In six months he was dead of lung cancer.

Propped against a wall of the milking room near the stainless storage tank stood eight or ten large portraits in heavy gilt frames of bearded men and stout, somber-faced women. They had been a kind of daguerreotype, the outlines emphasized by pen strokes, probably dating from the nineties or earlier. Once, Bert's oldest brother stopped by. The same mild face and cheerful greeting. He was a salesman for a local milking-machine dealer. I showed him through the much-remodeled house and he kept chuckling at his own total loss of recollection of how it had formerly looked. He was in his seventies then, hale and intelligent, but without much curiosity about the past: the massive old loom of chestnut wood I had discovered in the enormous attic; the spinning wheel; a couple of shoeboxes full of letters, grammar-school diaries, and notebooks belonging to his sisters, Bert, and himself. Like Bert, he seemed to feel all this stuff belonged to a dead-and-gone phase of life irrelevant to anything modern. When I offered him his family's portraits he looked at me in surprise and burst out laughing.

Of course he recognized his parents and grandparents, but the notion of retrieving their portraits from the barn was incomprehensible. I had the feeling, as with his brother, that the land and the house and barns were all little more than a work place, and outmoded at that. We might as well have been wandering about in some old factory from which he had managed to escape.

140

In one of the shoeboxes in the attic were picture postcards dated 1918, sent from Los Angeles, San Francisco, and a few other towns in northern California, addressed to his mother by Bert. Apparently he had been in the Army during the first War and had been assigned out there. A typical card read: "Am in Fresno. It is nice. Pie is ten cents, quart of milk seven cents, loaf of bread ten cents, coffee five cents." Or: "Am in Los Angeles. It is nice. Pie . . ."

Yet there must have been a time when the house and farm had had some less objectified meaning for the people living here. Across the front beside the road there still stood a row of seven enormous maples with some side branches twenty inches thick that had been planted for seven girl children at their births. The house itself was the precise replica of four others that face down into the bottom of the bowl-shaped valley, built by sons of Captain Tanner after he was mustered out of Washington's army. The Captain's house, situated on the highest elevation, was one foot larger in all dimensions. It burned down many years ago but the foundation is still there in the woods. They are all ample, even prepossessing houses built in the early 1800s, so the land had to have been agriculturally economic for at least a century or more. In the shoebox notebooks are essays by Tanner girls, faultlessly done in round Palmer method style, on the Egyptian pyramids, the Panama Canal, as well as the Constitution and other patriotic subjects. They would have been a few classes ahead of Bob Tracy in the one-room schoolhouse half a mile away.

Apparently some great change occurred in the twenties, to judge by alterations made in the classic house. The massive brick fireplace and its baking compartments were torn out sometime in that era. This according to Bert's older brother, who grinned with amusement at the new one I had installed, in order to stop drafts and the heat loss. In the twenties boom salesmen had gone around convincing these people that to be up to date they had to have kerosene heaters that would save the enormous amounts of time wasted in cutting wood and the space for storing it. Another improvement was an immense concrete porch stuck on the clean lines of the house front, a place to sit and watch the activity on the unpaved road, where, even in the fifties, two or three people might pass by in a day.

One way or another, they had wanted to catch up, although a document I found nailed to a timber in the milk room seemed to indicate a climax in their despair of ever doing so. It was a pink slip torn out of a state inspector's notebook, splotched with brown manure stains. The inspector had listed in pencil the violations of the Health Code he had apparently been warning about for some time past. "Temperature of the cooler is still too high. Floor drain must be opened up. Screens are torn, flies all around.'' Half a dozen other infractions followed, and at the bottom was the ultimatum: ''Will stop Friday for your intentions.''

Beneath this was a wide penciled scrawl written in such anger that the pencil point had torn the paper: ''Stick it up your ass.'' With this defiant flourish ended the domain of the revolutionary war captain.

The contents of the shoebox, some thirty tintypes, snapshots, and formal studio photographs dated no later than 1906, and leather postcards of the same era, are, with three or four exceptions, the evidence of a romantic sentimentality that Bert and his older salesman-brother certainly remembered and with which they ultimately broke without regrets. The men's faces uniformly express the Victorian style of rectitude and determination, the women frequently affect the slightly tilted head of demure femininity. But one snapshot shows a barefooted man in overalls standing a few feet from a woman who was probably his wife. His hair is uncombed and his grin is wry, while she stands with both elbows raised as she pours whisky out of a bottle into a glass. Behind them is a rough farmhouse with a low plank stoop and sheathing of unmilled planks. Then there is a full-figured man in a studio shot taken in Hartford; he has a stiff collar and cutaway jacket and high-topped shoes. Through the middle of his chest is a bullet hole that frayed the back of the heavy card paper on which the picture was printed. Whether someone hated him enough to shoot at his picture or whether it was merely set up as a rifle target for the hell of it is impossible to know.

To have built five solid, large houses within view of each other, the family must have thought it had a permanent future. The construction details are chaste, impeccably tasteful, made to endure. In contrast, a kitchen wing thrust out of the side of the house in the eighties was set on beams laid on bare earth, and these were rotted out by the time I took over. The chestnut-beamed living-room ceiling had been covered by sheets of embossed tin, and so many layers of wallpaper had been laid up that they stood three or four inches away from the walls. The windows had gotten so loose that clear plastic sheets had been taped to their insides and bellied into the room when the wind blew. A veritable brook ran through the dirt-floored basement and a stone in one corner of the foundation had been removed to let it run out. Yet only a few years before he sold out, Bert had reinforced the barn with cement blocks. Probably he couldn't make up his mind whether to stay or leave until his mother's death decided for him. The doors of the house open on gorgeous views of everlasting hills, but inside, the city man's illusions of rural stability, enduring values, and inner peace are just that, illusions of a continuity long since vanished.

142

10

He knows cement. Some who are not particularly partial to him claim there are one or two others who can beat him at laying up stone, but even they admit that nobody can touch him when it comes to cement. His detractors themselves can't walk onto a floor he has poured without noticing its perfection. "Who done this floor?" they will ask, and on hearing it was Rayburn they will glance around wondering how he manages to roll out cement like a carpet. If Rayburn had any interest in compliments on his work, however, the time is long past. Rayburn is interested in money, women, and hunting deer. With women and deer he has always had a symbiotic touch, but not with money. Of course he knows the reason—he and his wife spend too much. There are always three or four cars, the best scotch, a kitchen unnecessarily remodeled. But these are merely reasons that explain everything except the main thing, the mystery of why they never have any money.

It is a mystery, at least in part, because he so often does jobs for people who are not too bright, let alone shrewd, yet apparently have all kinds of money. Sometimes, in the middle of a job with the cement still wet, he has hiked his price for the hell of it, just to see if he can get away with it, and most often he is able to talk around his clients' complaints, getting what he asked for. This only deepens the mystery of his having so little and they, so easily overwhelmed, so much.

It only makes it worse that he looks like a success, a man so trim that common work clothes look tailored on him. On the job he wears a tan wide-brimmed hat tilted over his eyes, chino trousers with narrow cuffs nicely folded up above his boot tops, and a cigarette drooping from the corner of his mouth. Should the lady of the house emerge to watch him work for a moment, his two helpers wink; she usually remains to watch him move, with his flat-bellied torso so competent under a tightly fitted shirt. He faces the women who interest him with a front-and-center attention; he listens to women as though they were a kind of new music. Even standing still he seems in a forward motion that probably comes from working for so many years with drying cement. It is work that requires a lot of visual judgment, alertness, and an innate sense of time passing, qualities which can attract women when they, not cement, are the focus. No glance of his is vague or unseeing, an intensity which suggests deviousness to some people, even criminality, because he seems so to want whatever he glances at.

In the early fifties a short New York millionaire named Cummings appeared in the countryside, buying up several contiguous farms to combine them into a large stock-breeding place, and he called in Rayburn to pour the floors and foundations for his

147

new modern barns. As it happened, Rayburn was somewhat closer to financial desperation than usual. A year earlier, having decided to stop horsing around with his life, he tried to ride the new boom by subcontracting several overpass abutments for the interstate highway, then under construction. What with bank interest, rentals on immense machines, and the payroll for squads of workers, he had come out of it with nine thousand dollars in debts and feeling like a fool. When he heard Cummings' rolling basso voice on his phone, it was much more than a new job. According to the gossip, Cummings was majority stockholder in half a dozen national companies listed on the stock market. Most heart-lifting was the man's slurred and hesitant drawl, a manner of speaking that Rayburn had come to understand as the mark of extremely wealthy, elegant, and, as often as not, easily manipulated people when it came to cement.

Cummings surprised him. He had expected a tall, lean, tennis-playing type. Instead, he faced a short bullish man with an immense hard head and tiny blue eyes set close together and a big arched nose. Cummings, rather than offering gestures of equalitarian politeness, greeted him as an adversary he intended to watch. Besides, this job was not a swimming pool or a summer house. Among other things, there were to be bull runs whose concrete posts had to withstand the pressure of monsters, and Cummings commanded Rayburn's respect by demanding that all costs and specifications be submitted and in writing. When the time came to pour the barn floor, Cummings was out there in the cold of a November morning measuring the thickness of the concrete with a folding ruler. Notwithstanding his tweeds, his white unused hands, his salivary drawl, Cummings seemed to have not only money but competence and power. By the completion of the job, when Rayburn would normally have risen to supremacy over his usual employer and be on a first-name basis with him, Cummings was, if anything, still more remote than at the beginning. Without ever raising his voice, always polite, he maintained their adversary position as immovably as the commander of a battleship with his officers. Rayburn had never dealt with this kind of rich. The others had either put on a self-effacing veneer of democratic familiarity or lorded it over him. Cummings had class, and without apologies.

On the final day of the job, with the forms trucked away and the foundation back-filled with fresh earth, Rayburn walked alone over the vast concrete floor looking for any hairline cracks that may have opened as the slab settled, but there were none. From one end, where he stood for a moment, it looked like an aircraft runway in the middle of the open field, except for the two parallel troughs stretching most of its length. It would last, if not forever, then long after he was gone. He sometimes brought his wife Adele to look at big jobs like this, and he thought of bringing her to see this one. It was a goddamn perfect floor. He wished he had a camera to take a picture of it in the clear light of this faultless day. He kept meaning to get a Polaroid to record some of his jobs, except that nobody'd be likely to want to look at pictures of concrete. He remained standing there for a moment, not knowing why a feeling of sadness had come on him, a feeling of having been suckered. It happened like this often, he realized, once his men had gone and there was nothing left to do, and what he had made was suddenly no longer his. Well, screw it, in a couple of months the cows'll be shitting all over it anyway.

He walked up the rise to Cummings' house to pick up his check, pausing beside the Caddy convertible in the driveway when his eye caught the telephone hanging from the dashboard. Christ, they even make money while they're driving. A uniformed maid held the door half shut and looked frightened about letting him in, but Cummings appeared and he followed him into a small office at one end of the immense living room. The place, which he had known as a farmer's house, was unrecognizable, all yellow and blue now, smelling of some kind of airy perfume. The walls of Cummings' office were hung with pictures of horses, and three shotguns, worth a fortune to Rayburn's practiced eye, stood in a glass-front hardwood case. Cummings picked his check off the leather-topped desk and handed it to him.

The man was dressed now in a gray pin-striped suit and black wing-tipped shoes. "I've got to be at Kennedy by six," he said, the first personal remark he had made to Rayburn. "But I'll be back on the weekend. Are you married?"

"Yeah, I'm married," Rayburn said, and his instinct added, "but I can go anywhere."

"A group of us are putting up a condominium-type thing in Georgia, on the coast there. Another one in South Carolina. Like to talk to you if you think you could boss a thing like that."

"Any time, sure."

"I'll be in touch over the weekend."

Cummings turned and opened the office door. Rayburn longed to stay and talk about it; "boss a thing like that" had to mean twenty thousand a year. He walked around the desk toward the door, struggling to delay leaving, hot with the suspense. The break of his life. At the door, just as he was turning to say good-bye, his eye caught sight of a buck deer crossing over a stone wall not fifty yards away. His flesh was moving as he shook Cummings' hand, a contraction of muscle up along his spine. With a glance into the man's tiny eyes, he tried to fathom whether he had noticed the animal, but there was no sign, only the adversary distance as before.

Depending on her mood, his wife Adele either sulked or exploded when he set out to poach, but in the face of Cummings' job offer she was dumbfounded that Rayburn would even think of going after deer on his property. She was hardly up to her hus-

band's chin, a chain smoker with a manly stride, a good shot herself, a woman alternately fed up with and proud of her husband, who had more man in him than anybody she had ever met. He had been re-winning her for sixteen years, fleeing from her hard

150

body and returning again to subject himself to the rough common sense of the nurse she had once been. She followed him out of the house to the Pontiac, where he sat in the front passenger seat, his shotgun on the floor, waiting for her to get behind the wheel. Behind her stood the granite house he had built for them surrounded with thin gray birches.

"Chrissake, Del, he's gone to New York. There's nobody home but the maid."

"People like that prosecute," she said through the car window. "You going to stay sixteen years old forever?"

He sighed and leaned back in the seat to wait her out. She came around and got behind the wheel. The procedure was for her to let him off on the road, then to return for him in half an hour. If he had dropped a deer he would find Moe Dean or another friend, and after butchering the animal where it lay, they would drag the parts into Moe's pickup. The only moment of danger was immediately after the shot, at which time she would be innocently cruising the roads, and he on his way out of the area, taking care not to have a shell in his gun. An empty gun weakened any charge against him.

The sun had set. In the leafless woods on both sides of the road it was already dark. "I don't get it. I just don't get it. The man is offering you the chance of a lifetime. Or doesn't that mean anything to you?" She knew it was hopeless once he had glimpsed that horned crown moving.

He knew where to head for, an alfalfa field near the crest of a ridge overlooking Cummings' house below. He had hardly settled into a crouch behind a stone wall when the buck appeared, a perfect silhouette against the blue sky. The animal came to a halt twenty yards off, listened, then lowered its head to feed. Rayburn sighted, fired, and the animal died on its way to the ground. Discarding the empty shell, he stood up and started back the way he had come, through half-rotted woods and thorny blackberry bushes to the overgrown lumbering road at the end of which Del would be waiting on the paved road. He heard a shot and dropped to a crouch. His first thought was that another hunter was up here. In this darkness he could attract fire if he moved. He slid out of his crouch and onto the damp ground, turning his head in all directions. Anybody moving in the woods would make noise, but there was silence. It had to be someone out in the open field. That was odd; no hunter would be dumb enough to work out in the open.

Unless it was Cummings or a caretaker. He had heard of a caretaker but had never seen one around. A voice now, a voice calling out some kind of command, basso and rolling and furious. Rayburn had been caught twice by the police and had paid two twenty-five dollar fines. He reached into his jacket pocket for his two extra shells and threw them away. Brittle twigs over his head splattered in another blast. He went to his knees. Another blast, and on top of it, a fourth. The bastard was aiming lower now, trying to kill him. He reached out around him for the discarded shells, cursing.

152   *"I know you're in there. Come out or we're coming in."*

A moneyed rage, that propertied indignation which Rayburn had heard on other expeditions, foretold a court case that could put him in jail and make him ridiculous enough to harm his business. He had no fear of Cummings, merely hated him now for stealing his deer, but to be prosecuted by him was terrifying. Cummings could not be conned, Cummings would know no mercy. Rayburn drew his gun close, squeezed his feet up under him, and crouching low, ran through the brush at top speed, his trouser legs sawing through brambles. The basso shouting flew around him like gun blasts but there was no more firing, and once he had gained the lumbering road he walked, heaving for breath; by getting up and running he had challenged Cummings to fire low and hit him, but he hadn't dared. Rayburn laughed for an instant at having won out, but the thought of the buck being dragged off by others angered him, the thought of Cummings eating his meat.

If this sounds like fiction, there is no avoiding it; habitual deer jackers invite adventures. This one, however, had a flatter ending than some others Rayburn had been through. He had a phone call from Cummings next morning and met him in his office a day later. By this time he knew that Cummings had called in the state police, who had to have cast suspicion on him, since they had arrested him twice before. He appeared for the appointment anyway. Wearing clean chino trousers, a business-type felt hat, and leather zipper jacket and gloves, he entered the wealthy man's office and took a chair opposite him, removing his hat, unzipping his jacket, but keeping his gloves on rather than risk Cummings' noticing the raw lacerations on his hands from his rush through the brambles. With the office warm enough for Cummings to be sitting there in a broadcloth shirt, the gloves must have seemed odd to him. As Rayburn told it, Cummings merely questioned him about his experience running large projects and ended the interview promising to let him know his decision, and he, the mason, had got back into his Pontiac with a feeling of triumph marred only by the loss of his deer.

Actually, the suspicions planted in Cummings by the police had infuriated him; he felt he had dropped his guard with this man to whom he had offered an opportunity that should have won his gratitude. That Rayburn had promptly gone shooting on his land and now did not even deign to remove his jacket and gloves was incredible, a notification of his mocking disbelief in the generous offer. The fellow was merely making an appearance in order to show his brazen confidence that he could not be proven guilty.

They sat in silence. Having spent so many years working deals that required him to conceal his emotions, Cummings could only stare fiercely at the mason, his mouth clamped shut. Nor could Rayburn find a way to express his indignation at this millionaire who had robbed him of his deer.

For these reasons they never saw or heard from each other again.

153

MENS MOCCS

At the taxidermist's.

She is a dream-cow, but in more ways than one. The apple trees are untended, useless except for firewood, although doubtless gorgeous in their bloom and good to sit under for shade. She might be a family's milk supply in summer, but the cost of feeding her in winter makes her a luxury. She is beautiful, however, and mows the orchard quietly.

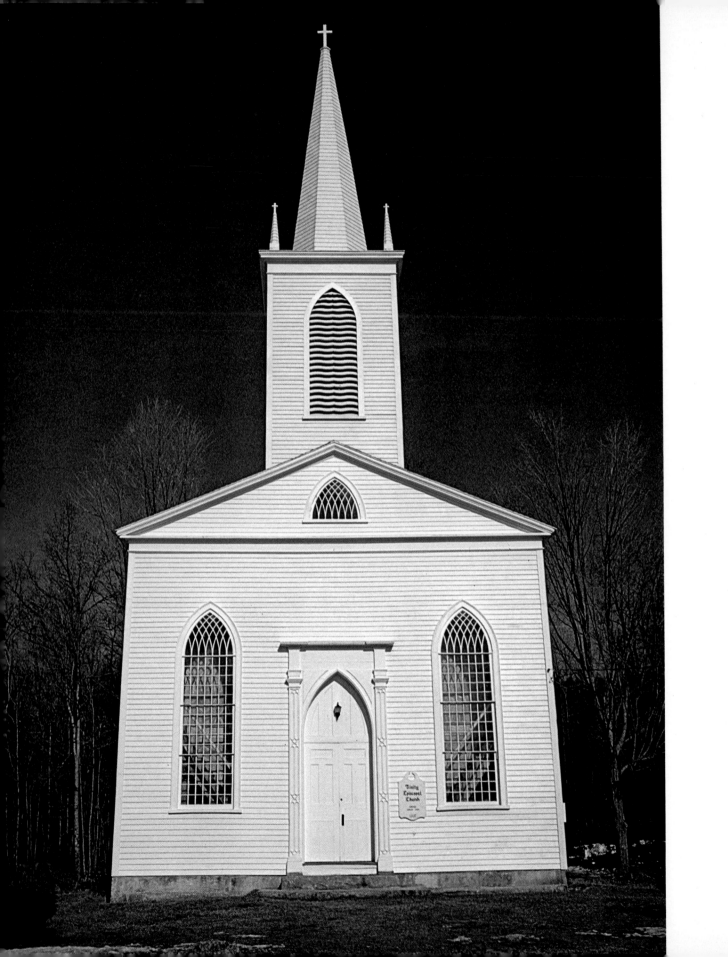

"... *like shards of a lost comity whose meaning is now read through the mists of nostalgia.*"

11

Most of our writing—and hence, our ideas of ourselves and society—is done in cities by city men and women. Yet our fundamental myths derive from country and village life, particularly the idea of each individual being somehow present in the leadership of government, personally represented, in effect. In spite of this, only a handful of people have ever met their mayor, even fewer their governor, and fewer still the president; moreover, it is a rare citizen who can tell you his congressman's name. A Chicagoan or a New Yorker held up in traffic by a hole being opened in the street will hardly wonder why he has not been consulted before the decision to dig was made. Driving to work one morning, he will discover that the toll on the highway he has traveled for years has been doubled, as if by magical forces beyond his furthest reach; calling a hospital he learns it has been closed. Not until his apartment burns is he likely to meet any of the firemen in his district, and if he is not a criminal or a giver of bribes he knows no policeman by sight or name. Nevertheless, he is by legend, myth, and even religion the master of his fate and the ultimate source of power. And if, as frequently happens, he lapses into depression or cannot identify himself any longer and goes insane, he is either drugged into a biological euphoria or taught to ransack his illusions about his relatives for a clue to his spiritual deprivation, they being the only people he has ever known at all.

Jefferson feared this alienation as a menace to republican government and for a long time tried to believe that the absence of a landless proletariat in America would keep her from European-style tyranny, but in his lifetime the city's domination had become obvious. Yet the dream hung on just as it had for Catiline and his class of ruined landholders overwhelmed by an urban Roman politics and culture, just as it had for the myth-infested mind of the Confederacy that saw itself as the last defense against the cash nexus and the impersonal rule of ruthless, mean, and value-blind city men. Like some ever-flowing underground river, the idea of the virtue of the man who works the land or lives close to its life-giving rule endlessly renews itself. There were cities when Genesis was written, and very old ones, but it is inconceivable that

Adam and Eve.

Paradise could be in any but a rural setting, and Cain, the first alienated man, is exiled not to a forest but to live east of Eden, among crowds of people.

If this age-old nostalgia for Eden is nothing more than an escape to an innocence that is itself suspect, nothing is lost in disposing of it as another human delusion. In any case, the majority of Americans—for the first time in history—live in cities now and will have to find salvation in the streets rather than on top of the ridge. To say that living on or near the land is substantively different is not necessarily to say that it is better for people than cities. For one thing, it is from the crowd that culture is made, however the crowd is despaired of or despised.

Whether I am better for it or not, I know that notions of connectedness occur to me which never could in a city. One morning recently, hearing the roar of heavy trucks on the road, I went out to investigate and found a double yellow line being painted down its center. I am acquainted with the man driving the truck, Clive Downs; he gave up farming ten years or so ago; his daughter won a couple of state-wide scholastic prizes, went to France on a grant to study at the Sorbonne, and married a French architect. The paint is fresh and I stand there hoping nobody comes along in a car to mar it before it dries. I find myself congratulating the Selectmen on the idea of painting a dividing line, having nearly skinned innumerable cars coming around the many blind turns on these narrow roads over the years. Finally, I wonder how much this is costing me in taxes, and even think to ask sometime whether the paint was purchased on competitive bidding. It all ends up being somehow my yellow line.

Some years ago a candidate for the office of Selectman convinced himself that one of the three town snowplows had disappeared and went about asking pointed questions about the honesty of an incumbent. A few days before the voting, the plow in question was set out on the town green with a hand-made sign on it reading, "Here is the missing plow." It turned out that the incumbent had taken it home, scraped it down, and painted it on his own time and at his own expense. But as little as the town has grown since, it is enough to make this kind of individual decision somewhat less likely.

Beside the road outside my first house there was a culvert concealed from view by weeds, and two guard posts to prevent cars from falling into it. One of the posts was rotten enough to fall over when hit by the wheel of my son's bicycle. I called Mr. Hurlbutt, then Town Clerk, and after a few weeks a crew of three men appeared and replaced the broken post. The foreman was a man in his sixties wearing a broad-brimmed straw hat and overalls. He was First Selectman then, equivalent to a mayor, and turned out to be one of the developers of mustard gas during the First World War, and now reputedly wealthy. I wiggled the remaining post to show that it might likewise be replaced. Then he wiggled it and each man in the crew tried his hand. Nobody contested that it wiggled, but the decision was unanimous that it merely needed the

170

earth packed around it more tightly, and this done everyone was satisfied it would last another winter. It did, but fell over in the following summer.

As one of those registered Democrats who never think of themselves as belonging to the party I had never attended a meeting of the Democratic Town Committee, so it was astonishing to be informed one morning in 1968 that I had been put in nomination for the post of delegate to the upcoming Chicago convention, and that I ought to show up at a meeting of the committee on the following night when a final vote would be taken. These were the days when outright opposition to continuing the Vietnam war was far from a majority feeling in the country, and certainly in the town as far as I was aware. I could only assume that some of the lonely doves scattered over the countryside had entered my name as a token protest.

The small two-story clapboard building that nobody quite dares call the Town Hall, at least not without a twinge of embarrassment, was fairly filled with some forty or fifty people seated on camp chairs in a semicircle at whose center sat the chairman and beside him my immediate neighbor, a farmer-Selectman whom I knew to be one of the Party Faithful, and, more important, a fanatic about keeping our roads cleared of snow. Under his administration certain hills were negotiable in January that, under previous Republican parsimony, were better left to skiers. It now transpired that he and I were in a dead tie for the delegate post, which he very much wanted for both the honor and the fun of going to Chicago free of charge, just as I wanted to stay home and finish work on a play I was writing.

Called on to explain our positions on the major issues, my opponent, as I barely recall, said very little, since all present were aware he would follow the Johnson-Humphrey leadership. In my turn I said what they also knew, that I was for McCarthy and a pullout from Vietnam, notwithstanding which I was ready to stand down in favor of my friend, who, apart from keeping the roads clean, had worked his head off over the years for any and all Democrats. Privately, I had no hope whatever that the McCarthy delegates could make a dent in the party's coming decisions, so that my election, apart from as minute an effect as propaganda against the war, seemed an injustice, however remote, to this long-time laborer in the party vineyards. In a word, I had been to Chicago more times than I wanted to remember; he never had been and wanted very much to go. They tallied themselves again and I won the honor by two votes. Dazzled by this unexpected dawning of a political career into which I had entered by attempting to exit, the embarrassing truth finally struck me. I had all but forgotten that actual living individuals are supposed to decide the fate of this country, and with enough determination might, from time to time, even manage to do so. Deferring to my friend was irresponsible and maybe worse, a surrender to cynicism about the democratic process itself.

Gift, seed-grown apple tree.

It was around the same time that a very young voice asked over my phone if I would donate a "Peace Tree" from a small nursery I operate to be planted in front of a nearby high school as a demonstration of the students' desire for an end to the war. A few days later, the same boy called to say that two other trees at other schools had been cut down during the night by patriots, and that the American Legion threatened to disrupt any ceremony with its howling members. Under the circumstances, his group thought that a new planting might only demonstrate how little opposition to the war really existed, so the offer was left in abeyance. As a compromise, he wondered if I would come and speak to an English class about *The Crucible*. The room was packed when I arrived. Faculty sat in a clump to one side. I had already learned that in inviting me to speak the students had struck terror in some faculty hearts, and the fear in the place was thick enough to grease a pan with. I thought I saw encouragement in a few faculty faces, but none of them joined the pounding applause of the students, all of whom knew about the canceled tree-planting. Their questions, clearly prearranged among them, were variations of the same one—whether I saw any connection between the hunting of witches and conditions in the present time.

Speaking of schools reminds me that the brand-new one, which three neighboring towns combined to build, irritates me whenever I pass it. Surrounded by hundreds of acres of open pasture and clumps of woods on a lovely rise with a miles-wide view, it has an Olympic-size swimming pool but few windows. False gambrel-like fronts stick up over the roof line, and best of all, the utility company sold the architects and the town on electric heat, and on grounds of economy, no less. The electric bills are climbing toward Pentagon-type figures. Part of my irritation stems from my own failure to attend the town meetings on the subject of the school, and the failure of several others who might have noticed some of its fatal incongruities before it was put up. I never thought of such things in the city, where one can only feel helplessness before public failures like this. In a small place one can at least connect such grave errors with one's own bad character, a help, however small, in disintegrating times.

Speaking of electric bills and public mistakes reminds me of a victory over the light and power company which could probably not have happened in quite the same way, if at all, in a big city. Since I had been brought up among crowds, the idea of a few individuals taking on a power company at all was not my idea of realistic behavior, but the fact is that a few dozen environmentalists, several years past, had succeeded in preventing the power company from stringing yet another set of high-tension cables and their pylons alongside an already cluttered state highway. At a power commission hearing, I delivered an aesthetic speech in praise of burying new electric cables underground, a speech which had been well publicized by a sympathetic press. Now, two years later, the power company had showed up with plans for a line of pylons, not over a highway, but within a thousand yards of my back door, as well as in the open country around my neighbors' homes. The company, moreover, was perfectly willing to sit down with the local people to discuss the new route, providing I was not invited to the meeting.

For most of the twenty or so people who gathered in a neighbor's living room to discuss how to fight the company, the new line of pylons over and around their homes was an affront. A doctor, a few professionals and small businessmen and retired folk, they had escaped from cities only to find themselves robbed of the natural scenery they had come here to enjoy. Some, however, were local workers whose hard-won property would be devaluated by the marching steel columns outside their windows. Significantly, the people in the nearby town of some five thousand were little exercised because, I suppose, they still had plenty of unspoiled country to gaze at on their Sunday drives. The farmers likewise were not upset; electric lines and progress are synonymous and besides, the company would pay something for its right of way and money earned without milking cows has a special emotional value, like finding a silver dollar at the bottom of a closet. It seemed an impossible fight, primarily because so few people were personally affected by the new scheme.

I supposed the company was banking on the sparseness of the opposition, but like me they had not reckoned with a retired engineer, Elmer Garrett, who lived in a wooded corner of the township. White-haired, soft-spoken, with a kindly smile and altogether a perfect model for a Norman Rockwell painting of a small-town pharmacist seated on a rocker with a cat on his lap, he quietly drew up calculations that, when presented before the power commission of the state, succeeded in convincing even the company's engineers that the new line was, quite simply, unnecessary and unjustified by the company's own projections of future demand. The project abandoned, Mr. Garrett returned to making hand-made paper in a nearby abandoned water-driven mill that he had reconstructed himself.

None of which proves anything at all, of course, as far as assurances for the future are concerned. The truth is that from the tip of Florida to the Canadian border, appearances of pasture and forest notwithstanding, the eastern seaboard is or will soon be one vast city and its suburbs. It is not merely a crowding into physical space but into the mind, a defensive isolation which more and more individuals feel themselves to be living in, that fracturing of community whose former coherence provided if not a just order then at least a palpable communal outline. Psychic security is not only a question of being able to leave one's door unlocked, but of knowing what to expect from strangers and neighbors in the ordinary course of existence.

12

There used to be a drunk in a nearby village, an odd-job man who, starting every Saturday afternoon, could be relied on to emerge staggering from the local tavern. By evening he would break into song and wander about past the windows of sleeping householders giving a roaring public concert until he collapsed somewhere, indoors or out, no one knew quite where. One evening, a widowed lady in her sixties returned to her empty home around midnight, and after getting into her nightgown in her dressing room, walked into her bedroom and turned on the light. There on her bed lay the fellow in question, fast asleep fully clothed, his two-day whiskers against her starched white pillow. Amazed and indignant, she shook him awake and demanded to know what he thought he was doing on her bed.

He opened his rheumy eyes, saw the lady, and yelled, "I was soooo *tired!*" She pointed down the stairs and he followed her finger out onto the road.

She had never met the man before, although she had heard about him and his drinking habits. Yet it apparently did not occur to her to make it a matter for the police, a forbearance which could have turned out to be a bad mistake, of course. What she did do was behave as though it were her house and her town and he simply had no right to be in her bed without asking permission. It is hard to imagine such confidence in a person less rooted in a place, a community, and hence in herself. The assumptions she made so unthinkingly would tend to dissipate in another kind of life, a life lived in an anonymous crowd.

But that incident is twenty years past and perhaps there are too many strangers around now to make quite the same reaction possible any more. Doors are locked which hadn't been since they were hung generations ago, and professionals cruise in

176

Overleaf: *Local talent.*

Farm interiors.

vans watching for the unattended house to cart away anything from guns to pianos. The procedure is for one man to be dropped off to reconnoiter. If he finds someone at home he asks directions and walks down the road to be picked up a short distance away; otherwise the van returns in a few minutes and they go to work. It is always done in daylight when a passing neighbor will most likely imagine a delivery is being made. Cars are stolen, if the keys are left in them, right out of the owner's driveway, and there is a thriving business in burglar-alarm systems. And once a place is robbed, the news spreads up and down the country roads, leaving in its wake, at least for a few weeks, a special bitterness and that familiar urban helplessness before human perversity, but it is probably made a little worse by its contrast with the surrounding beauty of the natural world and its perpetual promise of Eden.

That promise is most visibly smashed at the auctioning off of a farm's equipment when the place goes out of the business. Farmers are not noted for their sentimentality, and to be sure they come to an auction in hopes of making a good buy. The professional auctioneer, known to everyone in the crowd, is likewise emotionally uninvolved; his job is to squeeze the maximum price for each item. The numerable wisecracks with which he spices his spiel are familiar to the audience, which will allow him a return grin but rarely an outright laugh, their minds being totally joined to the tractor, the mower, the cow, or the cultivator that the unfortunately failed neighbor must dispose of.

The atmosphere is reminiscent of a funeral, and the humor likewise. It is not necessary for the farmer selling out to have gone bankrupt; quite the opposite sometimes —he may have made out pretty well by selling his land for a development. But if he has been a real, rather than a gentleman, farmer, there is a common understanding of a kind of mortality here, of a hope that has collapsed and of the shadow of that death approaching them as well. As vital as it is, farming is all but an anomaly now unless one has enormous capital. So the crowd of farmers will greet the man selling out with a certain sober dignity appropriate for one bereaved, and it is a genuine feeling, even as they are hoping to buy up his equipment as cheaply as possible. At one auction, the dividing line between these conflicting attitudes was reached.

As sometimes happens, a number of farmers had come to this auction from a distance away and were strangers to the locals. As one item after another went to buyers, it was obvious to the local men that the prices were indecently low. At some point in the sale, with no behind-the-scenes collusion, they began bidding up the prices—not outrageously, but to a level appreciably higher than that reached until now. It was a chancy operation, for if the strangers didn't bite, the locals who had bid high would be stuck. But they managed to lift the tone of the occasion and to a degree succeeded in raising the take without driving off the strangers altogether. When it was all over, nobody mentioned the matter at all. Nor was it a question of their admiration for the farmer who was selling out, a man who was by no means their idea of an exemplary practitioner of the agricultural profession. Quite the contrary, as a matter of fact. It was, rather, the idea of defeat which drew them together in his defense, their common awareness of the sweat that had gone into the place, and, if they did not applaud his methods of farming and would themselves have managed the place quite differently, they knew nevertheless that he had tried, and was worth their gesture of solidarity, mute and unconfessed as it might be, in this workless suburb of strangers that the country had become.

Halloween.

Overleaf: *The pet.*